W. A. Cole Albert Baur

College songs for Banjo

W. A. Cole Albert Baur

College songs for Banjo

ISBN/EAN: 9783744646642

Printed in Europe, USA, Canada, Australia, Japan

Cover: Foto ©Thomas Meinert / pixelio.de

More available books at **www.hansebooks.com**

Containing the leading College Songs

* AND POPULAR *

Songs of the Day.

College Songs FOR Banjo

ARRANGED BY | A. Baur, W. A. Cole, | AND OTHERS.

++ BOSTON: ++

COPYRIGHT, 1888, BY

-- Oliver Ditson & Company. --

New York: C. H. Ditson & Co.   Chicago: Lyon & Healy.   Philadelphia: J. E. Ditson & Co.

THE MARKET ON SATURDAY NIGHT.

By DAVE BRAHAM.

Arr. by A. BAUR.

1. I'm a poor mar-ket wom-an, I do a fine trade, A sell-ing my goods at the stall; .. A
2. Oh, the Mon-days and Tues-days and Fri-days are fine, The Wednesdays and Thurs-days are light; .. But
3. In the sum-mer or win-ter, oh, when the wind blows, A fill-ing wild dust all our eyes; .. In

nate bit of mon-ey me-self I have made, Where I eat with my back to the wall. ....
thou-sands of peo-ple all stand in a line, At the mar-ket on Sat-ur-day night. ....
rain or in frost or in ter-ri-ble snows, We are shout-ing and yell-ing our cries. ....

CHORUS.

1. We sell tur-nips and par-tridg-es, tur-keys and cab-ba-ges, Crock-'ry and tin-ware so
2. We sell lem-on's and but-ter beans, car-rots and hol-ly greens, Cel-'ry so crisp-y and
3. We sell pea-nuts, ba-na-nas, and Chi-nese ha-va-nas, Its real-ly a beau-ti-ful

bright; . It's par-snips and cress-es, and lit-tle babes' dress-es, At the mar-ket on Sat-ur-day night. .
white; . Oh, pick-les and chow-chow, and dogs that say "bow-wow" At the mar-ket on Sat-ur-day night. .
sight; . It's o-le-o-mar-ger-ine, little pigs and cro-beans, At the mar-ket on Sat-ur-day night. .

Copyright, 1888, by O. DITSON & Co.

LA PALOMA.

Composed by YRADIER.

Arr. for Banjo by GAD ROBINSON.

1. I think.......... of the morn when I sailed a-way from thee,   I said,...........
2. Ni'-na,............. when to shore re-turning thy smile I see,   My love...........
3. At last,........... on the shore we're landing, and grief has flown,   And there.........

.... "pray to God for me, pray to God for me,.............   I longed........ once more Ni-na's
.... for that time is yearning to com-fort thee,....... ....   And then........... I will quit for-
.... is my moth-er standing, but why a-lone?...........   Why does........... she with sor-row

sweet face and smile to view,..........   She sighed....... and she wept, when we said our sad a-dieu.
-ev-er the o-cean's breast,........   And ne'er........ from my dar-ling sev-er, but near her rest.
heed me, and not re-ply,...........   Why to........... this lone spot thus lead me with bit-ter sigh?

"Ni-na," said I, "if nev-er a-gain we meet,........ ...
Ni - na, to - mor-row let our wed-ding be,............
There in the churchyard ly-ing, a grave I see,............

Then shall a dove with white wings fly thee to
For I am come to thee, love, from o'er the
Ni-na that pure dove fly-ing, was thee, was

greet,.............
sea,.... ....
thee,.............

O-pen then wide thy win-dow, for it shall be,.............
Let then our hearts be light, and no more re-pine,.............
Sail-or boy, wake from sleep-ing, no long-er weep,.............

From heav'n a-bove, my soul which comes back to thee."........
For the pearl of the An-til-les shall be mine.........
You were the first watch keeping, and fell a-sleep.......
} Oh, the sail-or shall sing, O'er the waves as they

wing, When the breez-es are swaying and play-ing, But yet no ech-o bring, O'er the waves as they

wing, The gay sail-or shall sing, When the breez-es are.... swaying and play-ing, But yet no ech-o bring.

La Paloma.— 2.

GIVE ME THE WALTZ.

("PIPER HEIDSIECK.")

Tune Banjo to C.

Arr. by W. A. COLE.

1. Oh! some may sing of "Sweet Mo - selle,"— Of "To - paz,""Sher - ry," and of "Port," For
2. For sea - shore some may have a taste, And talk of roam - ing on the sands; But
3. Oh, 'tis the dance I love to see, It keeps me mer - ry all the year; What
4. It makes you ev - 'ry care for - get, It makes the dark - est hour seem light; The

some these things may do quite well, But as for me, they're not the sort. Give
as for me, 'tis plain to see The dream - y waltz un - ri valled stands. The
joy to glide so dream - i - ly With her, my lit - tle sweet - heart dear. Take
tru - est sport I've seen as yet, 'Mid all the fes - ti - vals of night. Give

me my charm - ing la - dy - love, With flash - ing eyes and spir - its gay, And
mu - sic seems to soothe my brain, And sings for me the sweet - est songs; While
moon - light ram - bles, if you choose, No pleas - ure in them can I see; But
me my charm - ing la - dy - love, With flash - ing eyes and spir - its gay, And

let us dance the dream - y waltz, Then care will quick - ly fly a - way.
all the joys of life a - gain Come flock - ing 'round in fai - ry throngs.
oh, to drive a - way the blues, Its waltz - ing, waltz - ing, boys, for me.
let us dance the dream - y waltz, Then care will quick - ly fly a - way.

CHORUS.

Oh, yes, give me the waltz, boys, That is the meas - ure, bring-ing such pleas - ure;

Oh, yes, give me the waltz, boys, That is the meas - ure for me, for me.

GIVE ME THE WALTZ.

8

BRING BACK MY BONNIE TO ME.

Arr. by A. BAUR.

Andante.
BANJO.

VOICE.

1. My Bon - nie lies o - ver the o - cean, . . My Bon - nie lies o - ver the sea; . . . . My
2. Last night as I lay on my pil - low, . . Last night as I lay on my bed; . . . . Last

Bon - nie lies o - ver the o - cean, . . Oh! bring back my Bon - nie to me. . . . .
night as I lay on my pil - low, . . I dreamt that my Bon - nie was dead. . . . .

CHORUS.
TENORS.

Bring back, bring back, Bring back my Bon - nie to me, to me;

BASSES.

BANJO.

Bring back, bring back, Oh, bring back my Bon - nie to me. . . . .

2nd Bar.

Copyright, 1888, by O. Ditson & Co.

LOVE, I WILL LOVE YOU EVER.

Composed by BUCALOSSI.

Arr. for Banjo by GAD ROBINSON.

1. Be-neath the trees to-geth - - er they wan - der'd hand in hand,..... (Oh!
2. Be-neath the trees to-geth - - er they went a - long a - part,....,. (Oh!

it was sum - mer weath - - er,) And love was in the land. Their
it was au - tumn weath - - er,) And heart was turn'd from heart. A-

hearts were light, the sun shone bright, And as they went a - long,...... With
-cross the wood the air came cold, The mists rose chill and gray,...... And

10

voic - es sweet - ly blend - ing, They sang the same old song......
in their ears like a mock - ing voice, They heard the well known lay.......

WALTZ.

Love, I will love you ev - - er, Love, I will leave you nev - -

- er; Ev - er to me Precious to be, Nev - er to part,

Heart bound to heart. Love, I will love you ev - - er,

Love, I will leave you nev - - er; Faith - ful and true,

Love, I will love you ever.— 3.

ev - er am I, Nev - er to say good - bye!

Yet, still while o'er the heath - er, They go their way a - lone,.... (Oh!

it is win - try weath - er,) And all the sum - mer's gone,...... They

hear the air they love the most, Up - on their fan - cy fall,....... "Tis

bet - ter to have lov'd and lost, Than not have lov'd at all.".......

Love, I will love you ever.— 3.

THOU ART MY OWN LOVE.

Arr. by A. BAUR.

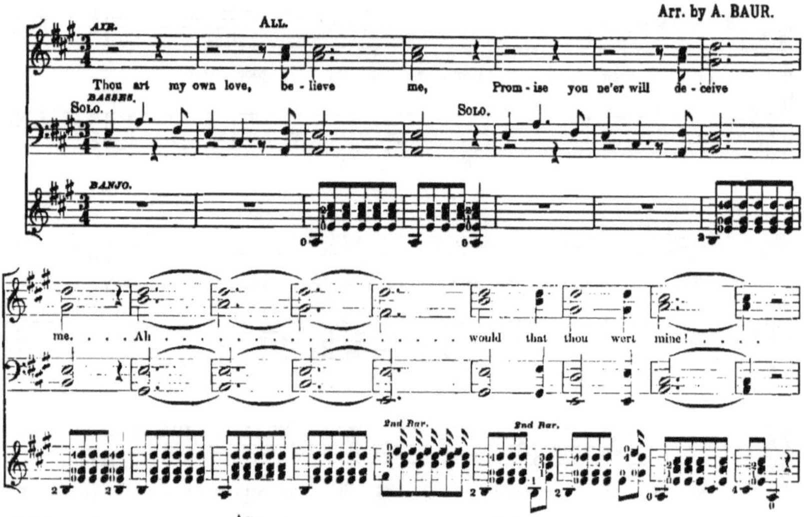

And oh, we'll dine on the fat of the land, O yes, we'll dine when we have

land, ...

mar - ried been, my love, when we have mar - ried been, my love, And oh, will dine on the

land . . . .

fat of the land, oh yes, we'll dine when we have mar - ried been.

land. . . . . . .

THOU ART MY OWN LOVE.

THE IRISH CHRISTENING.

By DAN MAGUINNIS.

ARR. by A. BAUR.

1. 'Twas
2. Th' aris-
3. There was

down in that place Tip - pe - ra - ry, Where they're so air - y and so con - tra - ry, They
toc - ra - cy came to the par - ty, There was Mc - car - ty light and heart - y, Wid
all sorts of tay, there was Schow - chong, And there was Ning - yong and there was Ding - Dong, Wid

cut up the dev - il's fi - ga - ry When they christened my beau - ti - ful boy; In the
Flor - ence Be - dal - ia Fo - gar - ty, (She says that's the French for her name). Di - o -
Oo - long and Too - long and Boo - long, And tay that was made in Ja - pan. There was

cor - ner the pi - per sat wink - in' and a blink - in' and a think - in', And a
ua - sus Al - phon - so Mul - roon - ey, oh! so loon - y and so spoon - y, Wid the
sweet-meats im - port - ed from Ja - va, and from Gua - va, and from Hav - re, In the

 Copyright, 1888, by O. DITSON & Co.

nag - gin of punch he was drink - in', And wish - ing the par - ents great joy.
charm - ing E - van - ge - line Moon - ey, Of so - ci - e - ty she was the crame.
four - mast - ed ship, the Mi - ner - va, That came from be - yant Hin - do - stan.

When home from the church they came with Fa - ther Tom, and big Mick - y Ban - ni - gan,
Co - ra Te - ra - sa, Maud Mc' - Cann, Al - ger - non Rouke and Lu - lu Mc - Caf - fer - ty,
Cowld ice - creams and cream that was hot, Ro - man punch froze up in snow - balls, spar - a - grass,

Scores of as par - ty a boys and girls as ev - er ye'd ax to see; When
Reg - i - nald, Mar - ma - duke Mau - rice Ma - gan, Clar - ence Ig - na - tius Mc - Guirk, Cor -
"Patte de foi gras," what - ev - er that manes, Made out of goose liv - ers and grease,

in flew the door, and Ho - gan the tink - er and Lath - er - ing Lan - ni - gan
ne - lius Hor - a - tio, Flah - er - ty's son, Ad - e - laide Grace and doc - tor O' Raf - fer - ty,
Red - head - ed ducks and sal - mon and peas, Ban - dy - leg'd frogs and Pe - ru - vi - an os - trich - es,

kick'd up a row, And want - ed to know why they wasn't ax'd to the spree.
E - va Mc - Lough - lin, Co - ra Mul - doon And Brig - a - dier Gen - er - al Burke.
bot - tle nosed pick - er - el, wood - cock and snipe, And ev - 'ry thing else that would plase.

THE IRISH CHRISTENING.

And the ba - by set up such a squall - ing and such a bawl - ing and cat - er - waul - ing, And the
They were danc - ing the Pol - ka Ma - zur - ka, 'twas a work - er, ne'er a shirk - er, The
Af - ter din - ner of course we had spa - king, there was hand - shak - ing, there was leave - tak - ing, In the

3rd Bar.

p

nurse on the moth - er was call - ing, There was a time "mon um ga joy!" The
var - so - vi - an - na La Turk - er, And the Pol - ka - row - dow was di - vine. They
cor - ner ould moth - ers match-mak - ing, Wid oth - er such in - no - cent sins; And we

3rd Bar.

pi - per his chant - er was dron - ing, and a groan - ing, and a moan - ing; The
march'd and then went in to lunch - eon; O such punch - in' and such crunch - in'! They were
drank a good health to each oth - er, then to each broth - er, then to each moth - er; But the

3rd Bar.

D.S. ℟.

ould wo - man set up the cron - ing, When they christened sweet Dan - ny the boy. . . . .
bu - sy as bees at the munch - in', Wid cof - fee, tay, whisk - ey and wine. . . . .
last toast I thought I would smoth - er; When they hoped that the next would be twins. . . . .

3rd Bar.

5th Bar. Last time.

THE IRISH CHRISTENING.

GOOD-NIGHT.

Arr. by A. BAUR.

1. Good - night, la - dies; . . Good - night, la - dies; . . Good - night,
2. Fare - well, la - dies; . . Fare - well, la - dies; . . Fare - well,
3. Sweet dreams, la - dies; . . Sweet dreams, la - dies; . . Sweet dreams,

la - dies, We're going to leave you now. . . Mer - ri - ly we roll a - long,

roll a - long, roll a - long, Mer - ri - ly we roll a - long, O'er the dark blue sea.

IN THE MORNING BY THE BRIGHT LIGHT.

By JAMES BLAND.

Arr. by A. BAUR.

1. I'm gwine a - way by the light of the moon, Want all the chil - dren for to
2. Go get a match and light that lamp, . Want all the chil - dren for to
3. I'll take my old ban - jo a - long, Want all the chil - dren for to

fol - low me; I hope I'll meet you dar - kies soon,
fol - low me; And show me the way to the Bap - tist camp,
fol - low me; In case the boys should sing a song,

Hal-le - hal - le hal - le - hal - le - lu - jah! So tell the broth - ers that you meet,
Hal-le - hal - le hal - le - hal - le - lu - jah! We'll have beef - steak and spare rib stew,
Hal-le - hal - le hal - le - hal - le - lu - jah! For no one has to pay no fare;

Want all the chil - dren for to fol - low me; That I will trav - el
Want all the chil - dren for to fol - low me; And nice boiled on - ions
Want all the chil - dren for to fol - low me; So don't for - get to

on my feet, Hal - le - hal - le - hal - le - hal - le - lu - jah!
dipped in dew, Hal - le - hal - le - hal - le - hal - le - lu - jah!
curl your hair, Hal - le - hal - le - hal - le - hal - le - lu - jah!

CHORUS.
f TENORS.

In the morn - ing, morning by the bright light, Hear Ga - briel's trumpet in the morn ing!

BASSES.

BANJO.

2nd Bar.

"FORSAKEN."

By KOSCHAT.   Arr. by A. BAUR.

1st and 2nd TENORS.

1. For - sak - en, for - sak - en, for - sak - en am I; Like a stone in the cause - way, my
2. A mound in the church-yard, that blos-soms hang o'er; It is there my love sleep - eth to

1st BASS.

1. For - sak - en, for - sak - en, for - sak - en am I; Like a stone in the cause - way, my
2. A mound in the church-yard, that blos-soms hang o'er; It is there my love sleep - eth to

2nd BASS.

BANJO.

20

bur - ied hopes lie; I go to the church-yard, my eyes fill with tears; And kneel-ing I
wak-en no more; 'Tis there all my foot-steps, my pas-sions all lead; And there my heart

bur - ied hopes lie; I go to the church-yard, my eyes fill with tears; And kneel-ing I
wak-en no more; 'Tis there all my foot-steps, my pas-sions all lead; And there my heart

weep there, Oh, my love, loved for years; And kneel-ing I weep there, Oh, my love, loved for years.
turn-eth, I'm for-sak-en in-deed; And there my heart turn-eth, I'm for-sak-en in-deed.

weep there, Oh, my love, loved for years; And kneel-ing I weep there, Oh, my love, loved for years.
turn-eth, I'm for-sak-en in-deed; And there my heart turn-eth, I'm for-sak-en in-deed.

FORSAKEN.

BAVARIAN YODLE.
(THE WATERFALL.)

Arr. by J. C. M.

Arr. by A. BAUR.

AIR. SOLO. YODLE. SOLO.

1. Down the mountain side Doth a streamlet glide, Tra la, ... In the sunniest spot stands a
2. There where water sweeps, And the chamois leaps, Tra la, ... Where the birdlings sing, and the

VOICE ACCOMP.

La, la, la, la, la, la,

BASS.

BANJO.

YODLE. f CHORUS. YODLE.

lit - tle cot, Tra la, ... In the gar - den there, Sits my sweet-heart fair, Tra la
yod-lings ring, Tra la, ... With my sweetheart kind, Is my heart and mind, Tra la

La, la, la, la, la,

In the gar - den there, Sits my sweet-heart fair,
With my sweetheart kind, Is my heart and mind,

la, la, la,

f CHORUS. p YODLE.

la, ... Gives me ma-ny a kiss that she'll nev - er miss, Tra la la. . . . . .
la, ... By my dar - ling's side let me e'er a - bide, Tra la la. . . . . .

la, la, la, la, la, Gives me ma-ny a kiss that she'll nev - er miss, Tra la la.
By my dar - ling's side let me e'er a - bide, Tra la la.

la, la, la, la,

By my dar - ling's side let me e'er a - bide,

Gives me ma-ny a kiss that she'll nev - er miss, Tra la la.

WHAT THE DICKY BIRDS SAY.

From "Erminie," by JAKOBOWSKI.
Tune Banjo to C.

Arr. by W. A. COLE.

Allegretto.

mf

1. I'm not a free a - gent like
2. When brought a - fore his beak-ship, my

a - uy of you, There's them as looks ar - ter my fate, ... I
ev - i - dence to give, I'm al - lus in a dread - ful state .... For

ask their ad - vice when I've sum - mat to do, Their care and at - ten - tion is
fear I'll have to go to a set - tle - ment to live, A pen - al one is sure to be my

great. .... When - ev - er I wish - es to steal from the night A few
fate. .... Now ju - ries ain't ve - ry well up to their job, They for

hours for use in the day, ... Be - fore that I knows I'm do - in' what's right, I
fear of con - fine - ment all day, ... The ver - dict a - gree on by spin - nin' a bob, At

Copyright, 1888, by O. Ditson & Co.

see what the dick-y birds say.

least, so the dick-y birds say.

Chirp, chirp, chirp, chirp,

Chirp, chirp, chirp, chirp,

in the shrill-est tone, .. Chirp, chirp, chirp, chirp, in a tongue of their

own; .. What their war - bles and twit - ters con - vey, Tak - ing stud - y and thought for a

mind can be bought To de - fine what the dick - y birds, the dick - y birds say.

Chirp, chirp, chirp.

When

WHAT THE DICKY BIRDS SAY.

SHOOL.

Arr. by A. BAUR.

1. I wish I was in Bos-ton cit-y, Where all the girls they are so pret-ty, If I
2. I wish I was on yon-der hill, For there I'd sit and cry my fill, And
3. I wish I was a mar-ried man, And had a wife whose name was Fan, I'd

did 'nt have a time 'twould be a pit-y, Dis-cum bib-ble lol-la boo slow reel.
ev - 'ry drop should turn a mill, Dis-cum bib-ble lol-la boo slow reel.
sing her a song on this same plan, Dis-cum bib-ble lol-la boo slow reel.

CHORUS.
AIR.

Shool, shool, shool I rool, Shool I shag-a rack shool a barb-a cool, The

SECOND.

Shool, shool, shool I rool, Shool I shag-a rack shool a barb-a cool, The

BASS.

BANJO.

first time I saw psil - ly - bal - ly eel, Dis - cum bib - ble lol - la - boo slow reel.

first time I saw psil - ly - bal - ly eel, Dis - cum bib - ble lol - la - boo slow reel.

5th Bar.

MEERSCHAUM PIPE.

Arr. by A. BAUR.

VOICE.

BASSES.

1. Oh, who will smoke my meerschaum pipe? Meerschaum pipe, Oh, who will smoke my meerschaum
2. Oh, who will wear my cast - off boots? Cast - off boots, Oh, who will wear my cast - off

BANJO.

BASSES.

pipe? Meerschaum pipe, Oh, who will smoke my meer - schaum pipe, When I am gone a -
boots? Cast - off boots, Oh, who will wear my cast - off boots, When I am gone a -

2nd Bar.

BASSES.

way? Al - lie Ba - zan, Pat - sey Mo - ran, Ma - ry McCann, Cann, Cann.
way? Al - lie Ba - zan, John - nie Mo - ran, Ma - ry McCann, Cann, Cann.

3 Oh, who will squeeze her snow white hand?
Allie Bazan! Johnnie Moran! Mary McCann!
Kazacazan, Yucatan, Kalamazoo!

4 Oh, who will kiss her ruby lips?
Allie Bazan! Johnnie Moran! Mary McCann.
Kazecazau, Yucatan, Kalamazoo, Michigan.
BAD MAN!!!

IT SHOWERED AGAIN.

By DAVE BRAHAM.

Arr. by A. BAUR.

1. The clouds they were low - 'ry, the rum - ble of thun - der Was shak - ing the vault of the
2. We talked of the weath - er, the rain kept a fall - ing, And Mur - phy's white awn - ing be -
3. The horse - cars were crowd - ed, the street was block - ad - ed With bug - gies and wag - ons, yet
4. The sky it grew dark - er, the el - e - ments war - ring, The thun - der of heav - en so

dark heav - y sky, When I met Ma - ry Ca - sey and said, "Come in un - der the
gan for to leak; Then we heard a loud voice in the bar - room a bawl - ing, 'Twas
Mur - phy did sing; "Oh," said I "love - ly Ma - ry, I'm a - lone and un - aided," Then
loud - ly did roar, While I said "Dear - est Ma - ry, your love I'm im - plor - ing, Then

awn - ing of Mur - phy's till the show - er goes by." Said she, "With great pleasure, I've plen - ty of lei - sure, I'm
Mur - phy him - self with his mu - si - cal squeak; He sang, oh, so brave - ly, "The last rose of sum - mer," The
on her first fin - ger I placed a gold ring; She blushed like a po - sey and bowed her head shy - ly, And
Mur - phy looked out with a smile from his door; Said I, "Ma - ry Ca - sey, don't take this for blar - ney, The

tremb - ling and ner - vous in fear of the rain; Oh, we've wait - ed and wait - ed till the
crowd gath-ered round for to hear the sweet strain; Then said Ma - ry, "Good bye, oh, sure
whis - pered, "Now Bar - ney, oh, what do you mane? For me moth - er has prom - ised sure me
name of Pat Reil - ly has giv - en me pain; Will you mar - ry me, loved one? then she

2nd Bar.   2nd Bar.

CHORUS.

storm has a - bat - ed," She start - ed to go, but it show - ered a - gain. Oh we've
now I must leave ye," She start - ed to go, but it show - ered a - gain.
hand to Pat Reil - ly," She start - ed to go, but it show - ered a - gain.
an - swered, "Yes, Bar - ney," The sun it came out and it cleared off the rain.

2nd Bar.

wait - ed and wait - ed till the storm has a - bat - ed, She start - ed to go but it show - ered a - gain.

4th

THREE CROWS.

Line each stanza before singing.

TENORS.

largo.

1. There were three crows sat on a tree, And they were black as crows could be.
2. Said one old crow un - to his mate, "What shall we do for grub to eat?"
3. "There lies a horse on yon - der plain, Who's by some cru - el butch - er slain."
4. "We'll perch up - on his bare back - bone, And pick his eyes out one by one."

BASSES.

BANJO.

ONLY TO SEE THEE, DARLING.

Composed by CAMPANA.

Arr. for Banjo by GAD ROBINSON.

1. On - ly to see thee, dar - ling,   On - ly to hear   thy voice,..........
2. Gone is the sun - Et fu - ture,   Vis - ions of joy   too bright..........

.... E - ven its faint - est whis - per,   Would make my
.... Now ev - 'ry gleam hath fad - - ed,   Van - ish'd in

heart re - joice.   Vain - ly I crave the sun - shine,
dark - est night.   Too late, a - las! I know thee,

Thy love would e'er im - part; Hop - ing to see thee
Ah, let my poor heart tell, Breathe out its bit - ter

loved one, Trust - ing thy faith - ful heart!
an - guish In that last word, fare - well,

CHORUS.

On - ly to see thee, dar - ling, On - ly to hear thy voice,..........

E - ven its faint - est whis - - - per Would bid my

last time rall. *pp*

heart re - joice............. On - ly to see thee, my love,............

Only To See Thee Darling.—a.

TWINKLING STARS ARE LAUGHING, LOVE.

Composed by J. P. ORDWAY.

Arr. for Banjo by GAD ROBINSON.

1. Twink - ling stars are laughing, love, Laughing on you and me, While your bright eyes look in mine,..... Peeping stars they

The accompaniment for Chorus can be played for first part, if the other is too hard.

Copyright, 1885, by Oliver Ditson & Co.

seem   to   be;   Trou - bles come   and   go, love,   Brightest   scenes must

leave our sight,   But   the star of hope, love,   Shines with ra - diant beams to-night.

CHORUS.

Twinkling stars are laughing,   love,   Laughing   on you   and   me,

While your bright eyes look   in mine, Peeping   stars   they seem   to   be.

2.

Golden beams are shining, love,
Shining on you to bless;
Like the queen of night, you fill
Darkest space with loveliness.
Silver stars, how bright, love?
Mother moon, in thronely might,
Gaze on us to bless, love,
Purest vows here made to-night.

Twinkling Stars are Laughing, Love.— 2.

AFLOAT.

By MARKS.
TUNE BANJO TO C.

ARR. by W. A. COLE.

1. A song ! a song ! with merry ding, dong, For the sail-or bold and brave, . . Who loves to roam the seas a-mong, A - far on the roll - ing wave, . . On the roll - - - ing wave, On the roll - ing wave.

2. A song ! a song ! with merry ding, dong, For the sail-or's lass a - shore, . . Who'll think of him the waves a-mong, When the winds and tempests roar, . . When the winds . . . . And the tem - pests roar, . . .

When winds blow high . . he trims the flow-ing sail, . . . And gai - ly steers his barque so free, ... With daunt - less heart . . he hails the fresh'ning gale, . . For his home is on the

With fond fare - well . . she waves a part-ing hand, . . To speed him o'er the wa - ters blue, ... And oft she'll pray . . be - side the wave-beat strand, That Heav'n will bear him

deep blue sea, ... On the deep, . . the deep blue sea, ... In
safe - ly thro', ... That Heav'n will bear him safe - ly thro, ... For
3rd Bar.
3rd Bar.
risoluto.
espress.
storm or calm . . his watch he'll bravely keep, . . While ten - - der tho'ts his heart em - ploy, ...
well she knows . the dan-gers of the main, . . And how. . . will beat her heart with joy . .
. . That nerve his arm . . as o'er the boundless deep . . He speeds. Ship a - hoy! . . Ship a -
. . When o'er the bay . . his barque appears a - gain, . . With a - hoy! land a - hoy! . . Land a -
a tempo.
hoy! . . . . A - float on the bounding tide, . . . A - float on the roll - ing wave, . . a -
A - hoy! . . A - float, a - float, a - float, afloat, a -
A - hoy! . . A - float, a - float, a - float, afloat, a -
Poco rit.

AFLOAT.

PADDY DUFFY'S CART.

By DAVE BRAHAM.

Arr. by A. BAUR.

1. The ma - ny hap - py eve - nings I spent, when but a lad, On Pad - dy Duf - fy's
2. We'd gath - er in the eve - ning, all hon - est work - ing boys, And get on Pad - dy
3. Oh, a mer - ry lit - tle maid - en, so nob - by, neat and coy, A smil - ing up at

lum - ber cart, quite safe a - way from dad; It stood down on the cor - ner, near the old lamp
Duf - fy's cart, for no one marr'd our joys; All seat - ed in the moon - light, laugh - ing 'mid its
Duf - fy's cart, up - on her sweet-heart boy; It made a jeal - ous feel - ing, a qui - et piece of

light, You should see the con - gre - ga - tion there on ev - 'ry sum - mer night.
rays, Oh, I love to talk of old New York, and of my boy - ish days.
chaff; But all in play it died a - way, and end - ed with a laugh.

Chorus.

Oh, there was Tom-my Dob-son, now a sen-a-tor; Bil-ly Flyn and
Oh, there was Hen-ry Glea-son, now a mil-lion-aire; Cur-ly Bob and
Oh, there was Lar-ry Thom-son was a chum of mine; Lem-my Freer and

John-ny Glyn, oh, they were killed in war; All mer-ry boy-ish com-rades,
Whit-ey Bob, they're liv-ing on the air; All mer-ry boy-ish com-rades,
Sam-my Greer, they died in for-ty-nine; All mer-ry boy-ish com-rades,

rec-ol-lec-tions bring, All seat-ed there in Duf-fy's cart on sum-mer nights to sing.

Chorus, after 1st and 3rd verses.

Twink-ling stars are laugh-ing, love, laugh-ing on you and me; ....

PADDY DUFFY'S CART.

While your bright eyes look in mine, Peep - ing stars they seem to be.

CHORUS, AFTER 3RD VERSE.

What's the mat - ter? she chews to - bac - co,

Lit-tle Fraud, ... Lit - tle Fraud, ... she's the dain - ti - est dar - ling of all, ...

um - ber - rellas, um - ber - rel - las,

.... Lit-tle Fraud, ... Lit - tle Fraud, ... oh the dain - ti - est dar - ling of all.

PADDY DUFFY'S CART.

Mc SORLEY'S TWINS.

By GUS. PHILLIPS.

Arr. by A. BAUR.

VOICE.

BANJO.
Lively.

1. Ar-rah Mrs. Mc Sor-ley had
2. Says Mrs. Mc Sor-ley, "A
3. Whin the christenin' was over the
4. Thin Mrs. Mc Sorley jump'd

fine pur-ty twins, Two fat lit-tle di-vils they were; . . . Wid shquallin' and bawl-in' from

christenin' we'll have, Just to give me two dar-lin's a name;" . . . "Faith, we will," says Mc Sor-ley, "sure

com-pany be-gun Wid good whis-key to fill up their shkins; . . . And the neighbors kem in just to

up in a rage, And she threaten'd Miss Mul-lin-see' life! . . . . Says ould Den-ny Mul-lins, "I'll

morn-in' till night, It would deaf-en you, I do de-clare. . . . Be me sowl, 'twas a cau-tion the

one they must get, Something grand, to be sure, for that same;" . . . Thin for god-mothers, Kate and Mag

wish a good luck To Mc Sor-ley's beau-ti-ful twins. . . . Whin ould Mrs. Mul-lins had

bate the firsht man That'd dar lay a hand on me wife!" . . . The Mc Gans and the Geoghans, they

way they would shcrame Like the blast of a fish-er-man's horn; . . . Says Mc Sor-ley "Not one bless-ed

Mur-phy stood up, And for god-fa-thers came the two Flynn's . . . Jo-han-na Ma-ria and Diag-

drank all her punch, Faith, her legs wouldn't hould her at all; . . . She fell flat on her shtomach on

had an ould grudge, And Mag Murphy pitched in-to the Flynns; . . . They fought like the di-vil, turned

CHORUS.

hour have I shlept, Since thim two lit-tle di-vils was born." . . . Wid de beer and the whis-key the
na-coius O' Mara, Were the names that they christened the twins. . . .
top of the twins, And they sot up a mur-ther-in shquall. . . .
o - ver the bed, And they shmothered the poor lit-tle twins. . . .

whole bless-ed night, Faith, they couldn't stand up-on their pins, . . . Such an il - le-gant time at the

christenin we had, Of McSorley's most beauti-ful twins.

INTERLUDE.

PEANUT SONG.

Arr. by A. BAUR.

VOICE.
SOLO.   CHORUS.

1. The man who has plen-ty of good pea-nuts, And giv-eth his neigh-bor none, . . He
Chorus. sha'nt have an-y of my pea-nuts, When his pea-nuts are gone; . . When his pea-nuts are
2. The man who has plen-ty of or - an-ges And giv-eth his neigh-bor none, . . He
Chorus. sha'nt have an-y of my oranges, When his or-an-ges are gone; . . When his oranges &c.

BANJO.

gone, . . When his pea-nuts are gone, He sha'nt have an-y of my pea-nuts When his pea-nuts are gone. . .

3 The man who has plenty of soft, sweet soda crackers,
   And giveth his neighbor none,
He sha'nt have any of my soft, sweet soda crackers,
   When his soft, sweet soda crackers are gone, etc.

4 The man who has plenty of ripe, red strawberry short cake,
   And giveth his neighbor none,
He sha'nt have any of my short cake
   When his short cake is gone, etc.

5 The man who has any salt junk,
   And will give his neighbor none,
He sha'nt have any of my salt junk,
   When his salt junk is gone, etc.

6 The man who has spondulacs
   And will give his neighbor none,
He sha'nt have any of my spondulacs
   When his spondulacs are gone, etc.

"EMMET'S LULLABY."

By J. K. EMMET.

Arr. by A. BAUR.

1. Close your eyes, Le- na, my dar-ling; While I sing your lul- la- by, fear thou no dan- ger, Le - na; Move not, dear Le - na, my darling, For your brooder watches nigh you, Le-na dear, An- gels guard thee, Le - na dear, my darling, Noth - ing e - vil can come near; Bright - est flow - ers bloom for thee, Darling sis- ter, dear to me, ...

2. Bright be de morn - ing, my dar - ling; Ven you ope your eyes, sun- beams glow all a - round you, Le - na; Peace be with thee, love, my darling, Blue and cloudless be the sky for Le-na dear, Birds sing their bright songs for thee, my darling, Full of sweet- est mel - o - dy; An- gels ev - er hov - er near, Darling sis- ter, dear to me, ...

CHORUS.

Go to sleep, Go to sleep, my ba - by, my ba - by, my ba - by, Go to sleep, my ba - by,

ba - by, oh, bye, Go to sleep, Le - na, sleep.

RUMSTY HO!

Arr. by A. BAUR.

SOLO. VOICE.

CHORUS.

1. A begger man laid himself down to sleep, Rumsty ho! rum - sty ho! A beg - ger man laid himself
2. Two thieves came walk - ing by that way, Rumsty ho! rum - sty ho! Two thieves came walk - ing
3. They stole his wal - let and they stole his staff, Rumsty ho! rum - sty ho! They stole his wal - let and they

BANJO.

down to sleep, By the banks of the Mer - sey so high and steep, Rum - sty ho! rum - sty ho!
by that way, And they came to the place where the beggar man lay, Rum - sty ho! rum - sty ho!
stole his staff, And then broke out in a great hoarse laugh, Rum - sty ho! rum - sty ho!

4 As I was going down Newgate stairs,
  Rumsty ho! rumsty ho?
As I was going down Newgate stairs,
I saw those two thieves saying their prayers,
  Rumsty ho! rumsty ho!

5 As I was going up Tyburn hill,
  Rumsty ho! rumsty ho!
As I was going up Tyburn hill,
I saw those two thieves hanging there still,
  Rumsty ho! rumsty ho!

THE QUILTING PARTY.

By FLETCHER.

Arr. by A. BAUR.

Andante.
VOICE.

1. In the sky the bright stars glit-tered, On the bank the pale moon shone; And 'twas
2. On my arm a soft hand rest-ed, Rest-ed light as o-cean foam; And 'twas
3. On my lips a whis-per trem-bled, Trem-bled till it dared to come; And 'twas
4. On my life new hopes were dawn-ing, And those hopes have lived and grown; And 'twas

BANJO.

from Aunt Di-nah's quilting par-ty I was see-ing Nel-lie home. . . .
from Aunt Di-nah's quilting par-ty I was see-ing Nel-lie home. . . .
from Aunt Di-nah's quilting par-ty I was see-ing Nel-lie home. . . .
from Aunt Di-nah's quilting par-ty I was see-ing Nel-lie home. . . .

CHORUS. *mf*

I was see-ing Nel-lie home, ... I was see-ing Nel-lie home; And 'twas

from Aunt Di-nah's quilt-ing par-ty I was see-ing Nel-lie home.

Repeat pp

JINGLE BELLS.

By J. PIERPONT.

Arr. by A. BAUR.

Allegro.

mf voice.

BANJO.

1. Dash-ing 'thro the snow, In a one-horse o-pen sleigh; O'er the fields we go, And
2. A day or two a-go, I thought I'd take a ride, And soon Miss Fan-nie Bright Was
3. Now the ground is white, Go it while you're young, Take the girls to-night, And

2nd Bar.

Laugh-ing all the way; . . Bells on bob-tail ring Mak-ing spir-its bright, What
seat-ed by my side; . . The horse was lean and lank; Mis-for-tune seem'd his lot, He
sing this sleigh-ing song, . . Just get a bob-tailed bay Two-for-ty for his speed, Then

CHORUS.

fun it is to ride and sing, A sleigh-ing song to-night. Jin-gle bells! Jin-gle bells!
got in-to a drift-ed bank, And we, we got up-set.
hitch him to an o-pen sleigh, And crack! you'll take the lead.

Jin-gle all the way; Oh, what fun it is to ride in a one-horse o-pen sleigh!

Jin-gle bells! Jin-gle bells! Jin-gle all the way; Oh, what fun it is to ride in a one-horse o-pen sleigh!

BINGO.

AS SUNG AT BROWN.

Arr. by A. BAUR.

SOLO.

1. The mil-ler's big dog. . lay on the barn floor, And Bin-go was his name; . .
2. They cut him up in-to sau - sage meat, And Bin-go was his name; . .
3. They whis-tled at. . that sau - sage meat, And Bin-go wagged his tail; . .
4. (*Whistle.* . . . .) And Bin-go wagged his tail; . .

TENOR.

1. 2. 3. Bin - go was his name; . .
4. Bin - go wagged his tail; . .

BASSES.

BANJO.

B - I - N - G - O,   B - I - N - G - O,   B - I - N - G - O,

B - I - N - G - O,   B - I - N - G - O,   B - I - N - G - O,

2nd Bar.

(Spoken by single voices.)
Omit in 4th verse, substituting the following.
1. 2. 3. Bin - go was his name, . . . B - I - N - G - O, Bin - go was his name. . . .
4. Bin - go wagged his tail, . . . B - I - N - G - O, (Omit in 4th verse.)
Ending for 4th verse.
Here's to good old Brown, drink it down, Here's to good old Brown, drink it down;
drink it down, drink it down,
Here's to good old Brown, she's the jol - liest place in town, Drink it down, drink it down, drink it down, down, down.
8th Bar.

A-ROVING.

Arr. by A. BAUR.

Allegro.
VOICE.

1 At num-ber three Old Eng-land square, Mark well what I do say; At
2. She was a girl a-pass-ing fair, Mark well what I do say; She
3. With love for her my heart did burn, Mark well what I do say; With

BANJO.

num-ber three Old Eng-land square, My Nan-cy does'nt she live there! I'll
was a girl a-pass-ing fair, And had dark blue eyes and curl-y hair; I'll
love for her my heart did burn, And I thought she loved me in re-turn; I'll

f Chorus.

go no more a-rov-ing with you, fair maid. A-rov-ing, a-rov-ing, Since
go no more a-rov-ing with you, fair maid.
go no more a-rov-ing with you, fair maid.

rov-ing has been my ru-i-in, I'll go no more a-rov-ing with you, fair maid.

4 But when my money was gone and spent,
　Mark well what I do say,
But when my money was gone and spent,
Then off on her ear away she went,
I'll go no more a-roving with you, fair maid.

5 By this I have a lesson learnt,
　Mark well what I do say;
By this I have a lesson learnt,
And I'll keep the money I have earnt
And go no more a roving with any fair maid.

TROUBADOUR SONG.

Music by GENEÈ.   Arr. for Banjo by GAD ROBINSON.

Why should I be, Thus full of glee, Tell me what day is this?..,........

Loud throb-bing heart, Thou dost at-test, How great my joy and bliss...........

Ah, 'tis Saint An - na, Saint An - na, Saint An - na,

No day so fair and dear In all the long, the glad, long year...............

An - na, to thee is my fav - 'rite way, My fav - 'rite way, my fav - 'rite way,

An- na, then Nan - nie, how sweet to say, How sweet to say, how sweet to say!

CHORUS.
a tempo.

An - na, for thee is my fin - est song, My fin - est song, my fin - est song.

An - na, I'll sing thee my whole life long, Yes, my whole life long........

CONSTANTINOPLE.

Arr. by A. BAUR.

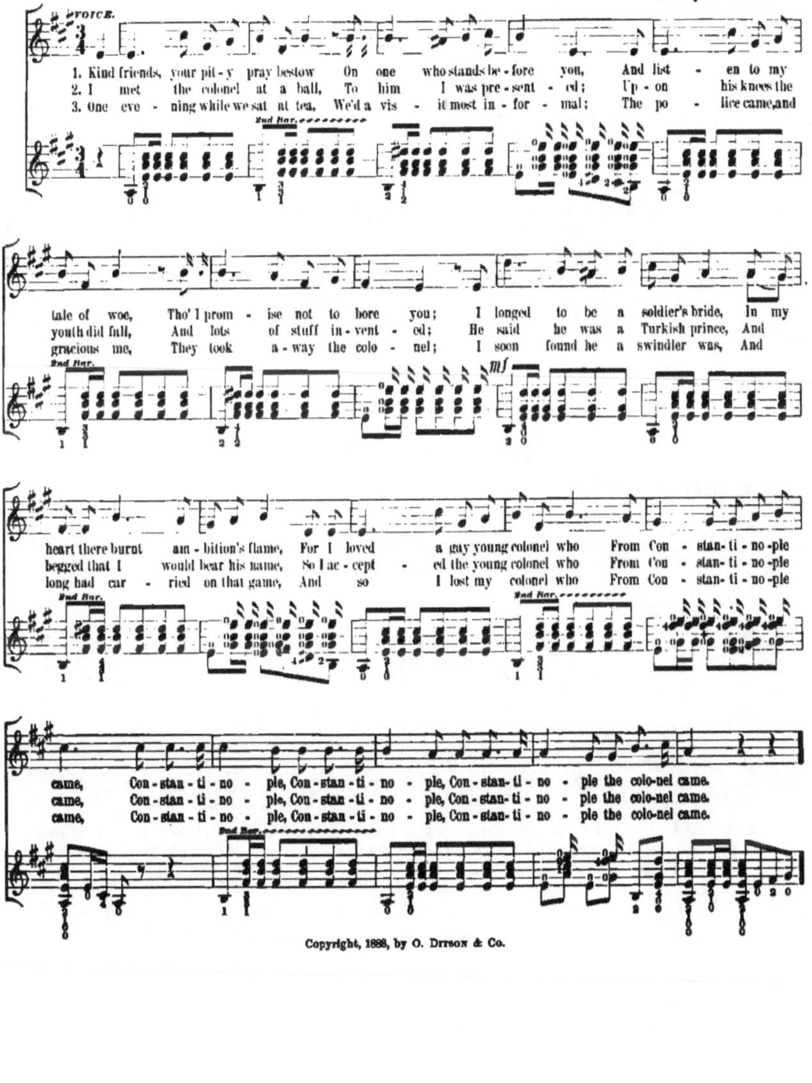

CHORUS.

C, O, N, with a con, with S, T, A, N, with a stan, with a con-stan, T, I, ti, with a con-stan-ti,

N, O, no, with a no, with a con-stan-ti-no, P, L, E, with a pull, Con-stan-ti-no - ple.

FAREWELL FOREVER.

By M. CONNELLY.

Arr. by A. BAUR.

1. All night thro' thy slum-bers my pas-sion-ate num-bers Have thrill'd to thy dream-ing
2. My heart, wild-ly beat-ing, would hear thee re-peat-ing Thy vow thou art mine a-

heart; / lone; Till drawn . . . . . by my sor - row, Thou wakst with the mor - row, To / And far . . . . . o'er the bil - low, My dream haunt-ed pil - low, Shall

poco agitato.

know that this hour we part, The dews of last night are dry on the / bring thee a - gain mine own, One touch on my hand, one kiss on my

ritard.

plain, Yet on my cheeks tears are fall-ing like rain. Oh! . . . . . . / brow, O - ver and thou art a mem-o - ry now.

Fare - well for - ev - er, Fare - well to thee, Moun - tains may sev - er man - y a

p ad lib. D.C.

lea; Bright tho' our dreaming, 'Twas not to be, Farewell, my own, to thee!

FAREWELL FOREVER.

MICHAEL ROY.

ARR. by A. BAUR.

Allegretto.

1. In Brook - lyn Cit - y there lived a maid, And she was known to fame; Her
2. She fell in love with a char - coal man, Mc - Clos - key was his name; His
3. Mc - Clos - key shout - ed and hollered in vain, For the don - key would - n't stop; And he

moth - er's name was Ma - ri Ann, And hers was Ma - ri Jane, And
fight - ing weight was sev - en stone ten, And he loved sweet Ma - ri Jane; He
threw Ma - ri Jane right o - ver his head, Right in - to a pol - i - cy shop, When Mc-

ev - e - ry Sat - ur - day morn - ing She used to go o - ver the riv - er, And
took her to ride in his char - coal cart On a fine St. Pat - rick's day, But the
Clos - key saw that ter - ri - ble sight, His heart it was moved with pit - y, So he

Chorus.

went to mar-ket where she sold eggs, And sau-sa-ges, like - wise liv - er. For oh! For oh! he
donkey took fright at a Jer - sey man, And started a' ran a - way.
stabbed the donkey with a piece of char-coal And started for Salt Lake Cit - y.

Shouted.

Repeat pp

was my dar - ling boy, For he was the lad with the au - burn hair, And his name was Mich - ael Roy.

Copyright, 1888, by O. Ditson & Co.

THE BOLD FISHERMAN.

Arr. by A. BAUR.

Tempo di valse.

VOICE.

1. There once was a bold Fish-er man, Who sail'd forth from Bil-lings-gate, To
2. First he wrig - gled then he strig - gled In the wa - ter so bri - ny 0, He
3. His ghost walked that ni - i - ight, To the bed - side of his Ma - ry Jane; He

BANJO.

2nd Bar.

catch the mild po - gy, And the shy mack - er - el; But when
bel - low'd and he yel - lowed Out for help but in vain, Then
told her how dead he was, "Then," says she, "I'll go mad, For

he ar - rived off Prim - li - co The storm - y wind it did be - gin to blow, And his
down did he gen-tly gli - i - ide. To the bot - tom of the sil - v'ry ti - i - ide, But
since my dov - ey is so dead," says she, "All jo - o - oy from me has fled," says she, "I'll

2nd Bar.

chant ad lib.

lit - tle boat it wib - ble wob - ble so, That slick o - ver - board he fell.
previous - ly to that he cri - i - ied, "Fare - well, Ma - ry Jane!"
go a rav - ing lu - ni - ac," says she, And she went star - ing mad.

SPOKEN AFTER FIRST VERSE.—All among the conger eels, and the Dover soles and the skipperred Herrings, and the Dutch plaice, and the White bait, and the Black bait, and the Tittlebats, and the Brickbats, and the Mullibobs, and the Rummy jobs. SINGING, *(Chorus after first verse.)*

SPOKEN AFTER SECOND VERSE.—When he came to the terra firma at the bottom of the aqua pura, he simply took a cough lozenge, and murmured, *(Chorus after second verse.)*

SPOKEN AFTER THIRD VERSE.—She thereupon tore her best chignon to smithereens, danced the "Can Can" on the top of the water butt, and joined the Woman's Rights Association; and frequently edifies the angelic members thereof by softly chanting a song of plaintive memory, viz. *(Chorus after third verse.)*

CHORUS. *f*

Twin - kle doo - dle dum, Twin - kle doo - dle dum, That's the high - ly in - ter - est - ing
Twin - kle doo - dle dum, Twin - kle doo - dle dum, That's the re - frain of the gen - tle
Twin - kle doo - dle dum, Twin - kle doo - dle dum, That's the kind of soul - in - spir - ing

D.C.

song be sung; Twin - kle doo - dle dum, Twin - kle doo - dle dum, Oh the bold Fish - er - man.
song be sung; Twin - kle doo - dle dum, Twin - kle doo - dle dum, Said the bold Fish - er - man.
strain she sung; Twin - kle doo - dle dum, Twin - kle doo - dle dum, Oh the bold Fish - er - man.

DUTCH WARBLER.

By SEP WINNER.

Arr. by A. BAUR.

Lively. VOICE.

BANJO.

1. Oh where, oh where ish my lit - tle dog gone; Oh where, oh where can he be? . . . .
2. I loves mine la - ger, 'tish ver - y good beer; Oh where, oh where can he be? . . . .

. . . . His ears cut short und his tail cut long, Oh where, oh where ish he? . . . .
. . . . But mit no mon - ey I can - not drink here, Oh where, oh where ish he? . . . .

3 Across the ocean in Germanie,
  Oh where, oh where can he be?
Der deitcher's dog ish der best companie,
  Oh where, oh where ish he?

4 Und sassage is goot, bolonie of course,
  Oh where, oh where can he be?
Dey makes em mit dog, und dey makes em mit horse,
  I guess dey makes em mit he.

DUTCH WARBLER.

ROSALIE.

Arr. for Banjo by GAD ROBINSON.

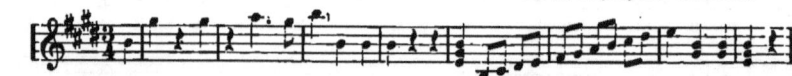

1. I'm Pierre de Bon ton de Par - is, de Par - is, I drink my di - vine Eau de vie, Eau de vie, As I
2. I go to the fête de Marquise, de Marquise, I go and make love at my ease, at my ease, I

ride out each day in my lit - tle cou - pé, I tell you I'm something to see..........
go to her père and de - mand for my own The hand of my sweet Ro - sa - lie..........

Chorus.

But I care not what oth - ers may say,......... I'm in love with Ro - sa - lie, Charming

Rose, pret - ty Rose,......... I'm in love with my Ro - - sa - lie..........

FUNICULI, FUNICULA.

Or, A MERRY HEART.

Words by E. OXENFORD.

Music by DENZA.

Arr. for Banjo by GAD ROBINSON.

1. Some think.......... the world is made for fun and frol - ic,..... And so do
2. Some think.......... it wrong to set the feet a - danc - ing,... But not so
3. Ah me!........... 'tis strange that some should take to sigh - ing,... And like it

I!............ And so do I!............ Some think.......... it well to
I!............ But not so I!............ Some think.......... that you should
well!.......... And like it well!.......... For me,............ I have not

be all mel - an - chol - ic,..... To pine and sigh,.......... To pine and sigh;.......
keep from coy - ly glanc - ing,.... Up-on the sly!.........., Up-on the sly!........
thought it worth the try - ing,.... So can - not tell!.......... So can - not tell!........

But I,.............. I love to spend my time in sing - ing.....
But oh,........... to me the ma - zy dance is charm - ing,.....
With laugh,........ and dance, and song, the day soon pass - es,.....

Some joy - ous song,.......... Some joy - ous song,............ To
Di - vine - ly sweet!........ Di - vine - ly sweet!............ And
Full soon is gone;.......... Full soon is gone;............ For

set............ the air with mu - sic brave - ly ring - ing,...... Is far from
sure - - - ly there is nought that is a - larm - ing,..... In nim - ble
mirth.......... was made for joy - ous lads and lass - es...... To call their

wrong!.. Is far from wrong!............. Lis - - ten!
feet!..... In nim - ble feet!.............. Lis - - ten!
own!.... To call their own!.............. Lis - - ten!

Lis - - ten! e - choes sound a - far!...... Lis - - ten! Lis - - ten!

Funiculì, Funiculà.—3.

e-choes sound a-far, Tra la la la, Tra la la la, Tra la la la, Tra la la la!

E-choes sound a-far! Tra la la la, Tra la la la! Lis - - ten,

lis - - ten, e-choes sound a-far!..... Lis - - ten, lis - - ten,

e-choes sound a-far! Tra la la la, Tra la la la, Tra la la la, Tra la la

la, E-choes sound a-far! Tra la la la, Tra la la la. la.

1st. *2d.*

Funiculi, Funiculi.—3.

SLAVERY'S PASSED AWAY.

By DAVE BRAHAM.

Arr. by A. BAUR.

VOICE.

BANJO.

2nd Bar.

1. Oh child, come to me and just
2. Oh child, in those times there I
3. Oh, I don't complain, it will

sit down by my knee, I'll tell that same old sto-ry just once more, Of
liv'd a-mong the pines, Yes, in an old log cab-in I was born, Then
nev-er come a-gain, So all our lit-tle chil-dren black and brown, They

2nd Bar.

dark cloud-ed years, Oh, so full of bit-ter tears, In those bond-age days of long be-fore the
I heard the moan when the moth-ers lost their own, In those bond-age days, oh thank the Lord they're
ne'er can be sold for that yel-low shin-ing gold, For sweet free-dom,child, she has put on her

2nd Bar.

war. In rice-field and in cane, there the black man felt the pain, The
gone. That i-ron chain and band, they grow rus-ty in this land, No
crown. She came here in the night, oh then might gave in to right, Old

2nd Bar.

2nd Bar.

dri - ver's whip it cut him ev - 'ry day;   Our good Lord a - bove, with His
more the blood-hound hold the slave at bay;   So we bend the knee to the
A - bra'm Lin - coln brought a - bout the stay;   So shout hal - le - lu, there's a

nev - er dy - ing love, Made that cru - el, cru - el slav - ery pass'd a - way,
Lord that made us free, For that cru - el, cru - el slav - ery pass'd a - way,
lot of work to do, For that cru - el, cru - el slav - ery pass'd a - way.

CHORUS.

SOPRANO & ALTO.

Oh, shout hal - le - lu - jah, Freedom ev - er rules the land, Go bend your knee, black peo-ple, for to pray; The

TENOR & BASS.

Oh, shout hal - le - lu - jah, Freedom ev - er rules the land, Go bend your knee, black peo-ple, for to pray; The

BANJO.

shac - kle and the band has fell from the bondsman's hand, And that cru - el, cru - el slavery's pass'd a - way.

shac - kle and the band has fell from the bondsman's hand, And that cru - el, cru - el slavery's pass'd a - way.

SLAVERY'S PASSED AWAY.

IMOGENE DONAHUE.

By WILLARD THOMPSON.

Arr. for Banjo by A. BAUR.

1. Lis - ten while I sing to you a - bout a maid - en fond and true, Whose
2. Im - o-gene's fa - ther near and far was known as the driv - er of a bob-tailed car, And he

name is Im - o - gene Don - a - hue, And she lives on Sil - ver street. She's en-
look'd with pride on this mu - si - cal star, His son - in - law to be. They were

gag'd to be mar - ried, and has prom - ised her hand To the ver - y swell lead - er of a
ver - y soon mar - ried in a styl - ish way, With this big brass band en -

big brass band, Whom all the girls think migh-ty grand, In his u - ni - form so neat.
gag'd to play, To cel - e - brate the wed-ding day Of Im-o-gene Don - a - hue.

CHORUS.

When on pa-rade the band would play the lat-est mu - sic of the day, And cu - pid's dart caus'd

man-y a heart to flut - ter as they pass'd, The lead - er glancing left and right to cap - ti - vate all

girls in sight,And the big bass drum goes bom bom bom for the lead-er of the mil - i - ta - ry band.

3 They'd scarce been married a month or two,
  When Imogene packed her trunk and flew
Away with a man she hardly knew
  Who was cross-eyed and knock-kneed ;
With his matrimonial knot untied—
  This leader pined away and died,
For the loss of his fickle hearted bride,
  Sweet Imogene Donahue.

"BINGO."

A MARCHING OR STREET SONG.

ARR. by A. BAUR.

CHORUS. *Tempo di Marcia.*

Here's to good old Yale, drink it down, drink it down, Here's to good old Yale, drink it down, drink it down. Here's to good old Yale, She's so heart-y and so hale, drink it down, drink it down, drink it down, down, down. Balm of Gil-e-ad, Gil-e-ad,

ff
Balm of Gil - e - ad, Gil - e - ad, Balm of Gil - e - ad, Way down on the Bin - go Farm. We
cres.
won't go home an - y more, We won't go home an - y more, We
won't go home an - y more, Way down on the Bin - go farm.
p
Bin - go, Bin - go,
Bin - go, Bin - go, Bin - go, Bin - go, Way down on the Bin - go Farm.
ff Spoken.
B - I - N - G - O. . . .
D.C.

MY PRETTY JANE.

Composed by H. R. BISHOP.

Arr. by H. C. DOBSON.

Andantino.

1. My pret — ty Jane, my pret-ty Jane............... Ah! nev-er, nev-er look so
2. But name the day, the wed-ding day,............... And I will buy, will buy the

shy, But meet me, meet me in the eve - ing, While the
ring, The Lads and Las - ses there in fa - vors And

bloom is on, is on the rye............. } The spring is wa - ning
vil - lage bell, the vil - lage bells shall ring !............

MY PRETTY JANE. Concluded.

fast,   my love,...... The corn...... is in...... the ear;   The

sum-mer   nights are   com - ing love, The moon shines bright and

clear,   Then pret - ty   Jane, my   dear - est Jane, Ah!

nev - er   look   so   shy,............ But meet   me, meet me in the

eve -   ning, While   the bloom, the bloom is on the rye!............

PUT ON YOUR BRIDAL VEIL.

By DAVE BRAHAM.

Arr. by A. BAUR.

1. The bells dey am a ring - ing, chim - ing, swing - ing; Hail! wel-come to the bride-groom, hail! De
2. The bride she am a blush-ing, gush-ing, flush - ing Hail! wel-come to the bride-groom, hail! Dere's
3. The bells dey am a chim-ing, rhym-ing, hy - men, Hail! wel-come to the bride-groom, hail! The

choir dey am a sing-ing, mu - sic fling-ing, Love, go put on your bri - dal veil;
li - lies wid de ros - es, pinks and po - sies, Love, go put on your bri - dal veil;
preach-er am a pray-ing, mu - sic play-ing, Love, go put on your bri - dal veil;

The bride's name's Nan - ny and she's just left mam-my, For to go put on her snow white
In - deed she's hap - py wid her ma and pap - py, As she's put-ting on her snow white
Oh, she's got re - lig - ion like a fan - tail'd pig - eon, For to go put on her snow white

Used by permission of Wm. A. Pond & Co.   Copyright, 1888, by O. Ditson & Co.

veil,   Oh, shout, oh, shout the old year out,   Hail to the bride-groom, hail!
veil,   Oh, shout, oh, shout the old year out,   Hail to the bride-groom, hail!
veil,   Oh, shout, oh, shout the old year out,   Hail to the bride-groom, hail!

CHORUS.

Love,   put on your or - ange blos-soms,   Love,   put on your long   white trail;   Love,

sweet wed-ding chimes   are   peal - ing,   Love,   put on your bri - dal   veil.   veil.

D.C.

PUT ON YOUR BRIDAL VEIL.

CO-CA-CHE-LUNK.

Arr. by A. BAUR.

SOLO. *VOICE.*

1. When we first came on this cam - pus, Fresh - men we as green as grass;
2. We have fought the fight to - geth - er, We have strug - gled side by side,
3. Some will go to Greece or Hart - ford, Some to Nor - wich or to Rome,
4. When we come a - gain to - geth - er, Vi - gin - ten - ni - al to pass,

BANJO.

Now as grave and rev - er - end sen - iors, Smile we o - ver the ver - dant past,
Brok - en is the bond that held us, We must cut our sticks and slide.
Some to Green - land's i - cy moun - tains, More, per - haps, will stay at home.
Wives and chil - dren all in - clu - ded, Wont we be an up - roar - ious class!

CHORUS. *AIR.*

Co - ca - che lunk che lunk che la - ly, co - ca - che lunk che lunk che lay, Co - ca - che lunk che lunk che la - ly,

SECOND.

BASS.

Hi! O chick a che lunk che lay.

2nd Bar.   1.   Last time.

VIVE L'AMOUR.

Arr. by A. BAUR.

1. Let ev-ery good fel-low now fill up his glass, Vi-ve la com-pag-nie, And
2. Let ev-er-y mar-ried man drink to his wife, Vi-ve la com-pag-nie, The
3. Come fill up your glass-es, I'll give you a toast, Vi-ve la com-pag-nie, Here's
4. Since all with good hu-mor I've toast-ed so free, Vi-ve la com-pag-nie, I

drink to the health of our glo-ri-ous cause. Vi-ve la com-pag-nie.
joy of his bo-som and plague of his life. Vi-ve la com-pag-nie.
a health to our friend, our kind worth-y host. Vi-ve la com-pag-nie.
hope it will please you to drink now with me. Vi-ve la com-pag-nie.

Vi-ve la, vi-ve-la, vi-ve-l'a-mour, Vi-ve la, vi-ve-la, vi-ve-l'a-mour.

vi-ve-l'a-mour, vi-ve-l'a-mour, vi-ve la com-pag-nie.

MARY · HAD A LITTLE LAMB.

Hobart Version.

Arr. by A. BAUR.

1. Ma - ry had a lit - tle lamb, lit - tle lamb, lit - tle lamb, Ma - ry had a lit - tle lamb,

2. It fol - low'd her to school one day, school one day, school one day, It fol - low'd her to school one day,

It's fleece was white as snow. And ev - ery where that Ma - ry went, Ma - ry went, Ma - ry went,

It was a - gainst the rule. It made the chil - dren laugh and play, laugh and play, laugh and play,

Union of all parts in this measure.
Ev - ery where that Ma - ry went, the lamb was sure to go. Bleat - ing of the lamb,
Made the chil - dren laugh and play, to see the lamb at school.
5th Bar.
Ba - a - a - ah, Ba - a - a - ah, Oh! aint I glad to get out the wilderness, get out the wil - der - ness,
Oh! aint I glad to get out the wilderness, get out the wilderness,
get out the wil - der - ness, Aint I glad to get out the wil - der - ness, Lean - ing on the lamb!
get out the wil - der - ness, Aint I glad to get out the wil - der - ness, Lean - ing on the lamb!
2nd Bar.

THE DRUM-MAJOR OF SCHNEIDER'S BAND.

By A. J. MUNDY.

Arr. by W. A. COLE.

Tune Banjo to C.

pp

1. So - gers march-in' oop de street   To mooeic grand   On ev'-ry hand;
2. Ven dey march-es to de vors   Dot band vill blay   Such mooeic gay;
3. Home dem so - gers dey have got;   De vor is done,   An' back dey come;

All de beoplea run to meet   And   vel - come Schneider's Band;   Proud-ly marchin' on pe -
Ven dem guns an' cannon roars,   Dot   band vill valk a - vay;   So - gers blen-ty you may
From their ranks was many shot,   From   Schneider's na - ry one;   Marchin' proudly as be -

fore,   He looks so grand   Mitt staff in hand,   See dot Ma-jor of de corps!   Dey
find   At death's command   Vill lend a hand;   Schneider he vill stay pe - hind,   An'
fore;   Mit staff in hand   He look so grand;   See dot conquer'r of de vor,   Herr

call 'em Schnei - der's Band. | Hear dem, | De beeples cheer dem | As dey draw near dem | Mit moosic
so vill Schnei - der's Band. | Hark now, | Dem cannon bark, now, | Dot sun vas dark, now, | Mit battle's
Schneider mit his Band. | Hear dem, | De beeples cheer dem, | Und la-ger beer dem | At ev-'ry

grand; | Dey blay so fine, now, | Dot Wacht am Rhine, now, | It sound soob-lime, now | On Schneider's
schmoke; | Dey have con-clood - ed | If dey get shoot - ed | Dey don't vas suit - ed, | Dot vas no
stand; | Dey feel so fine, now, | Mit beer un' vine, now, | Dot Wacht am Rhine, now | On Schneider's

Band, | Dot vas such boo - ly moo - sic fine, De deutch-en Wacht am Rhine. | But
joke; | An' so dey blay dot moo - sic fine, De deutch-en Wacht am Rhine. | But
Band, | Vill sound more bes - ser grand un' fine, De deutch-en Wacht am Rhine. | But

ven you beers dot moo - sic blay so sveet, | See dot Band a marchin oop de street,

THE DRUM MAJOR.

Vy it vas you tink dey blay so grand? Who it vas you tink dot leads dot Band? You hear de

moosic gay, You hear de beeples say It surely must be Schneider leads dot Band. You hear de

D.C. Last ending.

moosic gay, An' as dey march away, You know dot it vas Schneider leads dot Band.

BA-BE-BI-BO-BU.

Arr. by A. BAUR.

B - a - ba, B - e - be, B - i - bi, Ba - be - bi, B - o - bo, Ba-be-bi - bo, B - u - bu, Ba - be-bi - bo - bu.

SOLDIER'S FAREWELL.

By J. KINKEL.

Arr. by A. BAUR.

1. How can I bear to leave thee? One part - ing kiss I give thee; And
2. Ne'er more may I be - hold thee, Or to this heart en - fold thee; With
3. I think of thee with long - ing, Think thou when tears are throng - ing, That

then what - e'er be - falls me, I go where hon - or calls me, Fare -
spear and pen - non glanc - ing, I see the foe ad - vanc - ing, Fare -
with my last faint sigh - ing, I'll whis - per soft while dy - ing, Fare -

well, fare - well, my own true love, Fare - well, fare - well, my own true love.
well, fare - well, my own true love, Fare - well, fare - well, my own true love.
well, fare - well, my own true love, Fare - well, fare - well, my own true love.

IT'S A WAY WE HAVE AT OLD HARVARD.

The term "Harvard" can be changed to suit any College.

Arr. by A. BAUR.

1. It's a way we have at old Har - vard, It's a way we have at old Har - vard, It's a way we have at old Har - vard, To drive dull care a - way; . . To drive dull care a - way, . . To drive dull care a - way, ... It's a way we have at old Har - vard, It's a way we have at old

2. For we think it is no sin, sin, sir, To take the Fresh - men in, sir, And ease them of their tin, sir, To drive dull care a - way; . . To drive dull care a - way, . . To drive dull care a -

3. For we think it is but right, sir, On Wednesday and Saturday night, sir, To get most glo - rious - ly tight, sir, To drive dull care a - way; . . To drive dull care a - way, . . To drive dull dare a -

BASSES.

BANJO.

CODA.

Har - vard, It's a way we have at old Har - vard, To drive dull care a - way....

4 Brother Quidam is up in a pear tree,
Brother Quidam is up in a pear tree,
Brother Quidam is up in a pear tree,
  Io! io! io!
  Io! io! io!
  Io! io! io!
Once so merrily drinks he,
Twice so merrily drinks he,
Thrice so merrily drinks he
  Io! io! io!

5 Brother Quidam's a jolly good fellow,
Brother Quidam's a jolly good fellow,
Brother Quidam's a jolly good fellow,
  As all of us can say,
  As all of us can say,
  As all of us can say,
Once so merrily drinks he,
Twice so merrily drinks he,
Thrice so merrily drinks he,
  Io! io! io!

FINALE. The song is ended by the following stanza to the tune of "God save the Queen."
  So say we all of us,
  So say we all of us,
  So say we all.
  So say we all of us,
  So say we all of us,
  So say we all of us,
  So say we all.

OVER THE BANISTER.

Arr. by A. BAUR.

BARITONE SOLO.

1. O - ver the ban - is - ter leans a face, Ten - der - ly sweet and be - guil - ing,
2. No - bod - y on - ly those eyes of brown, Ten - der and full of mean - ing,
3. Holds her fin - gers and draws her down, Ten - der - ly grow - ing bold - er, Till her

la, la, &c.

MALE VOICES ACC'P'T ad lib.

BANJO ACC'P'T.

While be - low her, with ten - der grace, He watches the pict - ure smil - ing. The
Gaze on the lov - li - est face in town, O - ver the ban - is - ter lean - ing.
love - ly hair lets its mass - es down, Like a man - tle o - ver his shoul - der. A

light burns dim in the hall be - low, No - bod - y sees them stand - ing,
Tim - id and tir - ed with down - cast eyes, I won - der why she lin - gers,
ques - tion asked, a swift ca - ress, She has fled like a bird from the stair - way, But

Say - ing good-night a - gain, soft and low, Half way up to the land - ing,
Af - ter all the good - nights are said? Some-bod - y holds her fin - gers!
o - ver the ban - is - ter comes a "yes", That bright-ens the world for him al - way!

3rd Bar.

OVER THE BANISTER.

THE SPANISH CAVALIER.

By W. D. HENDRICKSON.

Arr. by A. BAUR.

Moderato.

1. A Span-ish cav-a-lier stood in his re-treat, And on his gui-tar play'd a
2. I am off to the war, to the war I must go, To fight for my coun-try and
3. And when the war is o'er, to you I'll re-turn, Back to my coun-try and

tune, dear; The mu-sic so sweet they'd oft-times re-peat, The bless-ing of my coun-try and you, dear.
you, dear; But if I should fall, in vain I would call, The bless-ing of my coun-try and you, dear.
you, dear; But if I be slain, you may seek me in vain, Up-on the bat-tle field you will find me.

Used by permission of GEO. W. HAGANS, San Francisco. Copyright, 1888, by O. DITSON & Co.

Say, dar - ling, say, when I'm far a - way, Some - times you may think of me, dear,

Bright sun - ny days will soon fade a - way, Re - mem - ber what I say and be true, dear.

RIG-A-JIG.

Arr. by A. BAUR.

1. As I was walk-ing down the street Heigh - o, heigh - o, heigh - o, heigh - o, A pret - ty girl I
2. Said I to her, "What is your trade?" Heigh - o, heigh - o, heigh - o, heigh - o, Said she to me, "I'm

RIG-A-JIG.

chanced to meet, Heigh-ho, heigh-ho, heigh-ho. Rig - a - jig, jig, and a-way we go, a-
weav-er's maid, Heigh-ho, heigh-ho, heigh-ho. Rig - a - jig, jig, and a-way we go, a-

way we go, a-way we go, Rig - a - jig, jig, and a-way we go, Heigh-ho heigh-ho heigh-

o, heigh-o, heigh-o, heigh-o, heigh - o, heigh - o, heigh-o, heigh-o, heigh-o,

Rig - a - jig, jig, and a - way we go, heigh-o, heigh-o, heigh-o.

NELLIE WAS A LADY.

By STEPHEN FOSTER.

Arr. by A. BAUR.

1. { Down on the Mis-sis-sip-pi float - ing, Long time I trab-ble o'er the way; }
   { All night the cot-ton wood I's tot - ing, Singing for my true lub all the way. }
2. { Now I'se un-hap-py and I'se weep - ing, Can't tote the cot-ton wood no more; }
   { Last night when Nel-lie was a sleep - ing, Death came a knocking at the door. }

Nel - lie was a la - dy, last night she died; Toll the bell for lub-ly Nell, my

dark Vir - gin - ia bride, Oh, Nel - lie was a la - dy, last night she died, Toll the bell for lub - ly Nell, my dar - key bride, my dar - key bride, Oh, Nel - lie was a la - dy,

last night she died, Toll the bell for lub - ly Nell, my dar - key bride. Nel - lie was a la - dy, she was;

After last verse.

last night she died, she did; Toll the bell for lub - ly Nell, my dark Vir - gin - ia bride, she was.

NELLIE WAS A LADY.

THE OWL AND THE PUSSY CAT.

By INGRAHAM.

Arr. by A. BAUR.

3rd time omit to 3rd verse.

1. The Owl and the Pus-sy cat went to sea in a
2. Pussy said to the Owl; you elegant fowl, How

beau-ti-ful pea-green boat; They took some hon-ey and plen-ty of money, Wrapp'd up in a 5 pound
charming-ly sweet you sing; O, let us be mar-ried, too long we have tarried; But what shall we do for a

note, The owl look'd up to the stars a-bove, And sang to a small gui-tar; O love-ly
ring? They sailed a-way for a year and a day, To the land where the bong tree grows, And there in a

Pus-sy, O Pus-sy, my love, what a beau-ti-ful Pussy you are! . . . .
wood, A Pig-gy wig stood with a ring at the end of his nose! . . . .

2nd Bar.   2nd Bar.

3. "Dear pig, are you will-ing to sell for a shil-ling your ring?" Said the Pig-gy, "I will." So they

took it a-way, and were mar-ried next day By the Tur-key who lives on the hill. They din-ed on mince and

slic-es of quince, Which they ate with a run-ci-ble spoon And hand in hand, on the

edge of the sand, They danced by the light of the moon. . . . .

Repeat pp

THE OWL AND THE PUSSY CAT.

DE GOLDEN WEDDING.

Words and Music by JAS. A. BLAND.
For Banjo by Geo. C. Dobson.

2d pos. Barre.

1. Les go to de golden wedding, All the dar-kies will be there; Oh, such danoing and such treading,
2. We will have ice-cream and hon-ey, Ap-ple bran-dy and mince pie; Darkies, wont it look too fun-ny,
3. Old Jim Grace will play the fid-dle, Beat the bones and old tam-bo, And Kersands will play the essence

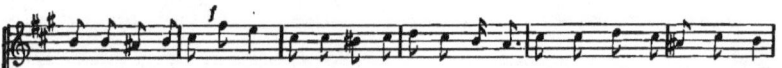

2d pos. Barre.

And such yel-low girls so fair! All the high-toned colored peo-ple That re-side for miles a-round,
When Aunt Di-nah does Shoo-Fly? Un-cle Joe and Hez-e-ki-ah From the old Car'-li-na state
On Jim Bo-bee's ole ban-jo, Mac In-tosh will kiss Lu-cin-da, Kase she is so ver-y shy,

Have re-ceived an in-vi-ta-tion, And they sure-ly will come down.
Will be at the Gold-en Wedding, Kase them col-ored gents am great.
And the lit-tle pic-ca-nin-nies, They will dance and sing Shoo-Fly.

2d pos. Barre.

Chorus.

All the dar-kies will be there, Don't for-get to curl your hair; Bring a-long your

Chorus.

damsel fair, For soon we will be tread-ing. Won't we have a jol-ly time,

Eat-ing cake and drinking wine? All the high-toned darkies will be at the Golden Wedding.

UPIDEE.

Arr. by A. BAUR.

VOICE.

1. The shades of night were fall-ing fast, Tral la, la, Tral la, la, As thro' an Al-pine vil-lage passed,
2. His brow was sad his eye be-neath, Tral la, la, Tral la, la, Flashed like a fal-chion from its sheath,
3. "Oh stay," the mai-den said, "and rest," Tral la, la, Tral la, la, "Thy wea-ry head up-on this breast."

BANJO.

ritard.

Tra la, la, la, la! A youth who bore,'mid snow and ice, A ban-ner with the strange de-vice,
Tra la, la, la, la! And like a sil-ver clar-ion rung The ac-cents of that un-known tongue,
Tra la, la, la, la! A tear stood in his bright blue eye, But still he answered with a sigh,

CHORUS.

U-pi-dee-i dee-i da, U-pi-dee, u-pi-da, U-pi-dee-i dee-i da,

U-pi-dee-i da. * r-r-r-r-r-r-r-r-r-r-r-r-r-r-r-r-r-r-r-r-r-r-r yah, yah, yah, yah.

At break of day as heavenward,
Tral la, la, tral la, la,
The pious monks of Saint Bernard,
Tral la, la, la, la,
Uttered the oft repeated prayer,
A voice cried through the startled air,
Chorus.

5 A traveller, by the faithful hound,
Tral la, la, tral la, la,
Half buried in the snow was found,
Tral la, la, la, la,
Still grasping in his hand of ice,
That banner with the strange device,
Chorus.

* Imitating a watchman's whistle.

OLD NOAH, HE DID BUILD AN ARK.

Arr. by A. BAUR.

1. Old No-ah, he did build an ark, Old No-ah he did build an ark.
   Old No-ah, he did build an ark, He made it out of hick-'ry bark.

If you be-long to Gid-eon's band, why here's my heart and here's my hand, Look-ing for a home.

2 He drove the anamiles in two by two, | Ter.
The elephant and the kangaroo.
Chorus.

3 And then he nailed the hatches down, | Ter.
And told outsiders they might drown.
Chorus.

4 And when he found be had no sail, | Ter.
He just ran up his own coat tail.
Chorus.

5 Full forty days he sailed around, | Ter.
And then he ran th' old scow aground.
Chorus.

6 He landed on Mount Ararat, | Ter.
Just three miles south of Barnegat.
Chorus.

7 O, Eve she did the apple eat, | Ter.
She smacked her lips, and said 'twas sweet.
Chorus.

8 When Adam walked the garden round, | Ter.
He spied the peelings on the ground.
Chorus.

9 And when he saw them, he looked blue, | Ter.
And vowed he'd have some apples too.
Chorus.

10 So he and Eve did strip the tree, | Ter.
And chanked away until they could see.
Chorus.

11 And then they saw how they'd got sold, | Ter.
In sucking down what Satan told.
Chorus.

12 And since old Brimstone sold them so, | Ter.
Most devilish sells have been the go.
Chorus.

13 Then keep your nose upon your face, | Ter.
It don't look well when out of place.
Chorus.

THERE'S MUSIC IN THE AIR.

Arr. by A. BAUR.

1. There's mu - sic in the air When the in - fant morn is nigh; And

1st TENOR.

2. There's mu - sic in the air .... When the noon-tide's sul - try beam Re -

ALTO.

3. There's mu - sic in the air .... When the twi-light's gen - tle sigh Is

BANJO.

faint its blush is seen On the bright and laugh - ing sky,

flects a gold - en light .... On the dis - tant moun - tain stream,

lost on eve - ning's breast, ... As its pen - sive beau - ties die,

Many a harp's ec - sta - tic sound, With its thrill of joy pro - found,

When be - neath some grate - ful shade, Sor - row's ach - ing head is laid,

Then, O then ' the loved ones gone, Wake the pure ce - les - tial song,

dim.   *2nd time* pp

While we list en - chant - ed there, To the mu - sic in the air.

Sweet - ly to the spir - it there Comes the mu - sic in the air.

An - gel voi - ces greet us there, In the mu - sic in the air.

OH, DEM GOLDEN SLIPPERS!

Arr. for Banjo by GEO. C. DOBSON.

Words and Music by JAMES A. BLAND.

1. Oh, my gold-en slippers am laid a-way, Kase I don't 'spect to wear 'em till my wed-din' day, And my long-tail'd coat, dat I loved so well, I will wear up in de chariot in de morn; And my long white robe dat I bought last June, I'm gwine to git changed Kase it fits too soon, And de gold-en slippers must be nice and clean, And yer age must be Just sweet six-teen, And yer

2. Oh, my ole ban-jo hangs on de wall, Kase it aint been tuned since way last fall, But de darks all say we will hab a good time, When we ride up in de chariot in de morn; Dar's ole Brud-der Ben and Sis-ter Luce, Dey will tel-e-graph de news to Uncle Bac-co Juice, What a

3. So, it's good-bye, children, I will have to go Whar de rain don't fall or de wind don't blow, And yer ulster coats, why, yer will not need, When yer ride up in de chariot in de morn; But yer

ole grey hoss dat I used to drive, I will hitch him to de char-iot in de morn.
great camp-meetin' dar will be dat day, When we ride up in de char-iot in de morn.
white kid gloves yer will have to wear, When yer ride up in de char-iot in de morn.

CHORUS.

Oh, dem gold-en slip-pers! Oh, dem gold-en slippers! Gold-en slippers I'm gwine to wear, Be-

cause dey look so neat; Oh, dem gold-en slip-pers! Oh, dem gold-en slippers!

1.　　　2.

Gold-en slip-pers Ise gwine to wear, To walk de gold-en street . . . . . . street.

LOVE.

Arr. for Banjo by EDMUND CLARK.

1. O Love it is such a ver-y fun-ny thing, It catches the young and the old, It's
2. When a man's in love with a ver-y pret-ty girl He talks as gen-tle as a dove, He
3. So boys keep a-way from the girls I say, And give them plen-ty of room, You'll

just like a chance in a lot-ter-y game, For ma-ny's the man's been sold, It will make you sing like a
calls her his honey and he spends lots of money, For to show her he's solid in love; When his money's all gone and his
think you're in clover till the honey-moon is over, And then you'll wish you were dead; With a cross-eyed ba-by

bird on the wing, It will cause your heart for to swell, You may love your wife as you do your life, But 'twill
clothes up the spout, He will find the old say-ing true, That a bird in the hand is worth two in the bush, What the
on each knee, With a wife with a wart on her nose, You will find that love don't run so smooth When you

em-pty your pock-et-book as well. So boys keep a-way from the girls, I say, And give them plenty of
dance is a fel-low going to do? With a wife and four-teen half starved kids I tell you it is no
have to wear your second hand clothes, When the rents are high the kids will cry, Kase they aint got nothing for to

room, You will find when you're wed they'll bang you till your dead, With the bald-head-ed end of a broom.
fun, When the butch-er comes round to col-lect his bills With a dog and a double barrell'd gun.
chaw, You'll hol-ler for your son for to load up the gun, For to vaccinate your mother-in-law.

CROW SONG.

Arr. by A. BAUR.

1. There were three crows sat on a tree, O Bil-ly Ma-gee, Ma-gar! There were three crows sat on a tree, O

2. Said one old crow un-to his mate, O Bil-ly Ma-gee, Ma-gar! Said one old crow un-to his mate, O
Bil-ly Ma-gee!

Bil-ly Ma-gee, Ma-gar! There were three crows sat on a tree, And they were black as crows could be, And they

Bil-ly Ma-gee, Ma-gar! Said one old crow un-to his mate, "What shall we do for grub to ate?" And they
Bil-ly Ma-gee!

all flapped their wings and cried, Caw, Caw, Caw, Bil-ly Ma-gee, Ma-gar! And they all flapped their wings and cried, Bil-ly Ma-gee, Ma-gar!

all flapped their wings and cried, Caw, Caw, Caw, Bil-ly Ma-gee, Ma-gar! And they all flapped their wings and cried, Bil-ly Ma-gee, Ma-gar!

"URALIO."

Arr. by A. BAUR.

SOPRANO & ALTO.

1. { When the ma - tin bell is ring-ing U - ra - li - o, ... U - ra - li - o, ...
   { From my rush-y pal - let springing, U - ra - li - o, ... U - ra - li - - - o. } Fresh as

morn-ing light forth I sal - ly, With my sick - le bright thro' the val - ley,

To my dear one gai - ly sing-ing, U - ra - li - o, ... U - ra - li - o. Fresh as - o.

WARBLE.
AIR.
La,
La,
VOICE ACCOMPANIMENT.
CHORUS.
BASS.
BANJO.
La,
URALIO.

THE DUTCH COMPANY.

Arr. by A. BAUR.

1. O when you hear the roll of the big bass-drum, Then you may know that the Dutch have come, For the
2. When Greek meets Greek, then comes the tug of war, When Deitch meets Deitch then comes the la - ger bier, For the

Deitch com - pa - ny is the best com - pa - ny, That ev - er came o - ver from old Ger - ma - ny.

Ho - ra - ho - ra, ho - ra, la, la, la, la, Ho - ra, ho, ra, ho - ra - tra - la - la - la, tra, la, la, la, lae, tra la, la, la, lae, . . He is mine oys - ter raw.

WABBLE.
AIR.

Tweed - leum, trie - trei, tru, trie, trei, tru, trie, trei, tru,

SECOND.
pp *fz* *fz* *fz*

Tweed - leum, trie - trei, tru, trie, trei, tru, trie, trei, tru,

BASSES.
pp

BANJO.

Tweed - leum, trie, trei, tru, trie, trei, tru, tra la - e - de - de.
fz *fz*

Tweed - leum, trie, trei, tru, trie, trei, tru, tra la - e - de - de.

THE DUTCH COMPANY.

THE BULL-DOG.

Arr. by A. BAUR.

1. Oh! the bull - dog on the bank, And the bull - frog in the pool, Oh! the
2. Oh! the bull - dog stooped to catch him, And the snap - per caught his paw, Oh! the

bull - dog on the bank, And the bull - frog in the pool. Oh, the bull - dog on the
bull - dog stoop'd to catch him, And the snap - per caught his paw. Oh, the bull - dog stoop'd to

bank, And the bull - frog in the pool, The bull - dog called the
catch him, And the snap - per caught his paw, The pol - ly wog died a

bull-frog A green old wa - ter fool, Sing - ing tra - la - la - la } la, la, la, ... singing
laughing, To see him wag his jaw, } leil - i - o, ...
tra - la - la - la { la - la - la, ... Sing-ing tra - la - la - la - la - la, sing - ing,
{ leil - i - o, ...
tra la, la, la, la, la, Tra la, la, la, tra, la, la, la, tra la, la, } la, la, la.
} leil - i - o.
Repeat pp

SERENADE.

By J. S. CAMP.

Arr. by A. BAUR.

Moderato.

AIR. BARITONE SOLO.

When op-press'd . . . by soft slum-ber, thine eyes thou slow - ly close, And I

1st & 2nd TENOR.

When oppress'd by soft slum-ber, thine eyes thou slow-ly close,

1st & 2nd BASS.

BANJO.

view thee calm be-fore me, so calm in thy re-pose, Thy

And I view thee be-fore me, so calm in thy re-pose, Thy

4th Bar. 3rd Bar.

fair lips mur - mur gen - tly art dream - ing, love, of me?

fair lips mur - mur gen - tly, art dream-ing, love, of me?

2nd Bar.

Dream

dolce.
Dream on, be - lov - ed, dream on, Yes, dream on for -
on, be - lov - ed, dream on, be - lov - ed, dream on, for -
dream on, Yes, dream on, be - lov - ed mine, ...
ev - er, dream on, be - lov - ed, dream on, for -
ev - er,
2nd Bar. 2nd Bar. 4th Bar. 5th Bar.
. . . dream on, for - ev - er, be - lov - ed mine. . . . .
ad lib.
legato.
ev - er, dream on, for - ev - - - - - - - - - er, be - lov - ed mine.
5th Bar. 5th Bar.

SOLOMON LEVI.

By FRED SEAVER.

Arr. by A. BAUR.

Allegretto.

1. My name is Sol - o - mon Le - vi; at my store on Sa - lem Street, That's where you'll buy your coats and vests, And ev - 'ry thing that's neat; I've sec - ond hand - ed ul - ster - ettes, And ev-'ry-thing that's fine, For all the boys they trade with me, At a hun-dred and for - ty - nine.

2. And if a bum - mer comes a - long to my store on Sa - lem Street, And tries to hang me up for coats, And vests so ve - ry neat; I kicks the bummer right out of my store, And on him sets my pup; For I won't sell clothing to an - y man Who tries to set me up.

CHORUS. UNISON.

O, Sol - o - mon Le - vi! Le - vi, tra, la, la, la! Poor sheen - y Le - vi!

Tra, la, la, la, la, la, la, la, la, la. My name is Sol-o-mon Le-vi, At my

store on Sa-lem Street; That's where you'll buy your coats and vests, And ev-'ry-thing else that's

neat; tra, la, la, Sec-ond-hand-ed ul-ster-e-ties, and ev-'ry-thing else that's

fine, For all the boys they trade with me, At a hun-dred and for-ty-nine.

IS THAT YOU, MR. REILLY?

By PAT ROONEY.

Arr. by A. BAUR.

1. I'm Ter - ence O' Reil - ly, I'm a man of re -
2. I'd have noth - ing but I - rish - men on the po -

nown, I'm a tho - rough - bred to the back - bone, ... I'm re - la - ted to O'
lice, Pat-rick's Day will be the Fourth of Ju - ly, ... I'd get me a

Con - nor, my moth - er was Queen Of Chi - na, ten miles from Ath - lone, ...
thou - sand in - fer - nal ma - chines, . To teach the Chi - nese how to die; . . . . .

But if they'd let me be, I'd have Ire - land free, On the
I'll de - fend work-ing-men's cause, Man - u - fact - ure the laws, New

Copyright, 1888, by O. Ditson & Co.

rail - roads you would pay no fare. . . . . I'd have the U -
York would be swim - ming in wine, ... A hun - dred a

nit - ed States un - der my thumb, And I'd sleep in the Pres - i - dent's chair. . . . .
day, will be ver - y small pay, When the White House and Cap-i-tol are mine. . . . .

Spoken after 1st verse.—I was walking across the Atlantic Ocean the other day, and as I was coming in the dock a fellow says: Cho.
Spoken after 2nd verse.—As I was walking quietly along the Elevated Railroad the other day, a gang of people below hollered up: Cho.

CHORUS.

1st time p, 2nd time f.
Is that Mis - ter Reil - ly, can an - y one tell? Is that Mis - ter

Reil - ly that owns the ho - tel? Well if that's Mis - ter Reil - ly, they speak of so

high - ly, Well, up - on my soul, Reil - ly, you're do - ing quite well. well.

Is that you, Mr. Reilly?

ALMA MATER O.

Arr. by A. BAUR.

1. We're gath-ered now, my class-mates, to join our part-ing song, To
2. No.. more for us yon tune-ful bell shall ring for morn-ing prayers, No
3. We.. go to taste the joys of life, like bub-bles on its tide, Now

pluck from memory's wreath the buds which there so sweet-ly throng; To
more to long Bi - en - ni - al we'll mount yon at - tic stairs; Our
glit - ter-ing in its sun-beams and danc-ing in their pride; But,

gaze on life's broad ruf - fled sea, to
re - ci - ta - tions all are passed, A -
bub - ble - like, they'll break and burst, and

which we quick-ly go, But are we start we'll drink the health of Al - ma Ma - ter O.
lum - nus - es, you know, We'll swell the prais - es long and loud of Al - ma Ma - ter O.
leave us sad, you know, There's none so sweet as mem - o - ry of Al - ma Ma - ter O.

4 Hither we came with hearts of joy, with joy we now will part,
And give to each the parting grasp, which speaks a brother's heart;
United firm in pleasing words, which can no breaking know,
For sons of Yale can ne'er forget their Alma Mater O.
Oh! Alma Mater O, Oh! Alma Mater O,
But ere we start we'll drink the health of Alma Mater O.

5 Then brush the tear-drop from your eye, and happy let us be,
For joy alone should fill the hearts of those as blest as we;
One cheerful chorus, ringing loud, we'll give before we go,
The memory of college days and Alma Mater O.
Oh! Alma Mater O, Oh! Alma Mater O,
Hurrah! Hurrah! for college days and Alma Mater O.

THE LAUTERBACH MAIDEN.

By BOETTGER.

Arr. by A. BAUR.

Tempo di valse.

VOICE.

BANJO.

1. In Lau - ter - bach hab' i mein'n strump ver - lor - en   Und
2. In Lau - ter - bach hab' i mein schuh erl ver tanzt,   Ohn'
3. In Lau - ter - bach hab' i mein her - zel ver lor'n,   Ohn'
4. Bin alle mein Leb tag nit trau rig ge - west,   Und

1. At Lau - ter - bach late - ly my stock - ing I lost,   With -
2. At Lau - ter - bach I danced the soles off my shoes,   Without
3. At Lau - ter - bach late - ly my heart I've lost,   With -
4. In all my life-time I have nev - er felt sad,   And for

oh - ne strump geh' i nit heim. . . .   Drum geh' i erst wie - der nach
schuh erl geh' i nit nach haus. . . .   Da steig ich dem schus - ter fen -
Her - zel da geh' i nit heim. . . .   Drum geh' i erst wie - der nach
bin a zum Trau - ern zu jung. . . .   Hab im - mer die Jung - en recht

out it I can - not go home; . . . .   To get me an - oth - er at
shoes I can't en - ter my house; . . . .   So I climb the cob - bler's
out it I feel quite a - lone; . . . .   Hence I must now re - turn to
griev - ing my years are too few; . . . .   Have al - ways loved to

Lau - ter - bach rein, Und hol' mir mein strump zu mein Bein. . . . .
Fen - ster hin - ein, Und hol' mir ein'n new - en her - aus. . . . .
Lau - ter - bach rein, Und hol' mir ein Herz zu mein'n Kein'm. . . .
ger - ne ge - seh'n, Und gro - sse und klein - ne ge - nung. . . . .

JODELN.

Lau - ter - bach, To - mor - row I thith - er will roam. . . . .
win - dow at once, To take new ones for my-self and my spouse. . . . .
Lau - ter - bach, To get me a heart for now I've none. . . . . .
flirt with the lads, With big and with lit - tle ones too. . . . . .

INTERLUDE.

D.S.

SCHLUSS.

FINE.

THE LAUTERBACH MAIDEN.

CARVE DAT POSSUM.

By SAM LUCAS.

Arr. by A. BAUR.

1. De pos - sum meat am good to eat, carve him to de heart; You'll
2. I reached up for to pull him in carve him to de heart; De
3. De way to de pos - sum sound, carve him to de heart; First

al - ways find him good and sweet, carve him to de heart; My dog did bark and went to see,
pos - sum he be - gan to grin, carve him to de heart; I car - ried him home and dressed him off
par - boil him, den bake him brown, carve him to de heart; Lay sweet po - ta - toes in de pan,

carve him to de heart, And dar was a pos - sum up dat tree, carve him to de heart.
carve him to de heart, I hung him dat night in de frost, carve him to de heart.
carve him to de heart, De sweet - est eat - in' in de lan', carve him to de heart.

CHORUS.
TENORS.

Carve dat pos-sum, carve dat pos-sum, chil-dren, Carve dat

BASSES.

BANJO.

pos-sum, carve him to de heart. Oh! carve dat pos-sum.

carve dat pos-sum, chil-dren, Carve dat pos-sum, carve him to de heart.

CARVE DAT POSSUM.

ANGEL GABRIEL.

By J. E. STEWART.

Arr. by A. BAUR.

1. Oh! my soul, my soul am a gwine for to rest In de arms of de an-gel Ga-bri-
2. Oh! my soul, my soul am a gwine for to rest, Gwine to rest just as sure as I
3. Oh! I shan't weep when I'm gwine for to leave, So I'll pack up my band box and I'll

el, And I climb on a hill, and I look to de west, And I
bo And I'll look like a black-bird a sitt'n on a rest, When old
go, And my breth-ren, oh! heark-en, and don't ev-er grieve, For I'm

cross o-ver Jor-dan to de Lam'l And I'll sit me down in de
Ga-briel am blow-ing on de horn; And I'll leave my clothes safe up-
gwine up to glo-ry ver-y slow; And I'll eat my meals, yes, three

old arm chair, Oh, brud-ders, I will nev-er tire; And old
on de shore, For I'll have new gar-ments for to wear; And I'll
times a day, Oh! you bet your life I went be late; And I'll

Sa - tan may sneeze, but I will take my ease, And I'll warm my-self at the ho - ly fire. . . .
have bran new shoes and nev - er get the blues, And be an - gels dey will come and curl my hair. . . .
have lots of fun, when you, my breth-ren, come, For I'm gwine to take de tick - ets at de gate. . . .

CHORUS.
I will shout, . . . And I'll dance, ...

I will shout, And I'll dance, And I'll wake up ear - ly in de morn, And

I will a - rise, and rub my sleep - y eyes, When old Ga - bri - el am blow - ing his horn.

ANGEL GABRIEL.

OH, MY DARLING CLEMENTINE.

By MONTROSE.

Arr. by A. BAUR.

Verse lyrics:

1. In a cav - ern, in a can - on E - ca - vat - ing for a mine, Dwelt a min - er, for - ty - nin - er, And his daugh - ter, Cle - men - tine.

2. Light she was, and like a fai - ry, And her shoes were num-ber nine, Her - ring box - es, with - out top - ses, San - dals were for Cle - men - tine.

3. Drove the duck-lings to the wa - ter, Ev - 'ry morn - ing just at nine, Hit her foot a - gainst a splin - ter, Fell in - to the foam - ing brine.

Chorus.

SOPRANO.
Oh my dar - ling, Oh my dar - ling, Oh my dar - ling Cle - men - tine, You are

ALTO.
Cle-men-tine, Cle-men-tine, Cle-men, Cle-men - tine, Cle-men, Cle-men -

TENOR.
Cle - men -tine, Cle - men -tine, Cle - men, Cle - men - tine, Cle - men, Cle - men -

BASS.
Oh Cle-men-tine, Oh Cle - men - tine, Oh Cle - men, Cle - men - tine, Cle - men, Cle - men -

BANJO.

lost and gone for - ev - er, Dref - ful sor - ry, Cle - men - tine.
tine, Cle - men - tine, Cle - men - tine, Cle - men, Cle - men - tine.

tine, Cle - men - tine, Cle - men - tine, Cle - men, Cle - men - tine.
tine, Cle - men - tine. Oh Cle - men - tine, Oh Cle - men, Cle - men - tine.

INTERLUDE.

5th Bar.

4 Ruby lips above the water,
  Blowing bubbles soft and fine,
  Alas for me! I was no swimmer,
  So I lost my Clementine.
        Chorus.

5 In the church-yard near the canon,
  Where the myrtle doth entwine,
  There grow roses and other posies
  Fertilized by Clementine.
        Chorus.

6 Then the miner, forty-niner,
  Soon began to peak and pine;
  Thought he "oughter jine" his daughter,
  Now he's with his Clementine.
        Chorus

7 In my dreams she still doth haunt me,
  Robed in garments soaked in brine;
  Though in life I used to hug her,
  Now she's dead I'll draw the line.
        Chorus.

OH, MY DARLING CLEMENTINE.

FAIR HARVARD.

Arr. by A. BAUR.

1. Fair Har - vard! thy sons to thy ju - bi - lee throng, And with bless - ings sur - ren - der thee
2. To thy bowers we were led in the bloom of our youth, From the home of our in - fan - tile

o'er, . . . By these fes - ti - val rites, from the age that is past, To the age that is wait - ing be -
years, . . . When our fa - thers had warned, and our moth - ers had prayed, And our sis - ters had blest, thro' their

fore. . . . O rel - ic and type of our an - ces - tor's worth, That has long kept their mem - o - ry
tears. . . . Thou then wert our par - ent, the nurse of our souls, We were mould - ed to man - hood by

warm, First flow'r of their wil - der - ness! star of their night, Calm ris - ing thro' change and thro' storm.
thee, Till freight - ed with treasure tho'ts, friendships, and hopes, Thou didst launch us on Des - ti - ny's sea.

3 When as pilgrims we come to revisit thy halls,
    To what kindlings the season gives birth!
Thy shades are more soothing, thy sunlight more dear,
    Than descend on less privileged earth.
For the good and the great, in their beautiful prime,
    Through thy precincts have musingly trod,
As they girded their spirits or deepened their streams
    That make glad the fair city of God.

4 Farewell! be thy destinies onward and bright!
    To thy children the lesson still give—
With freedom to think, and with patience to bear,
    And for right ever bravely to live.
Let not moss, covered error moor thee at its side.
    As the world on truth's current glides by,
Be the herald of light, and the bearer of love;
    Till the stock of the Puritans die.

www.ingramcontent.com/pod-product-compliance
Lightning Source LLC
Chambersburg PA
CBHW030625270326
41927CB00007B/1316